MW00609108

IN THE COMPANY OF
POETS

Dionis with baby Cynthia on her shoulders

Dionis Coffin Riggs was my mother. We had a special bond, she and I. She was the youngest of four daughters by twelve years. I was the youngest of three daughters by six. We were New Englanders to the core, our family. No overt declarations of affection. Not much hugging, no kissing. A respect for personal space. Yet all-encompassing, intense, seldom acknowledged love enveloped all of us, my parents, my sisters, and me. Love came in glances, in smiles, in gestures. And in poetry. My mother poured out the love she felt for the sea, the Island, the trees and flowers and seasons and scents. For us, her daughters. For her husband, our father. In several of her poems she tells of the frustration she feels as she sees beauty, feels love, but can only express it in poetry. She would cherish this anthology, which includes some powerful poems. All, even the most unlikely, she would recognize as having been created by love.

—Cynthia Riggs

A note about the illustrations: Sidney
Noyes Riggs (American, 1892 – 1975),
in his pursuit as a printmaker worked
on an extensive series of linoleum
block prints featuring many well-known
locations and buildings on Martha's
Vineyard after retiring to his Martha's
Vineyard family home in 1954. His
illustrations also were used by his wife,
Dionis Coffin Riggs, in many of her
books. A collection of his prints can
be found at the Martha's Vineyard
Museum.

ISBN: 978-0-9975846-4-6

CONTENTS

CLEAVELAND HOUSE POETS
1963-2021

Ellie Bates

Barbara Bradley

Jane Brown

Nan Bryne

Ruth Cochrane

Joe Eldridge

Janet Holladay

Russell Hoxsie

Robert T. Hyde

Bob Kaplan

Francesca Kelly

Peter Ledermann

Christopher Legge

Marion Lineaweaver

Lee H. McCormack

Don McLagan

George Mills

Georgia Morris

Judith Neeld

Katrina Nevin

Nora Nevin

Fan Ogilvie

Randall Pease

Kathryn Leonard-Peck

Susan Puciul

Andrea Quigley

Arnie Reisman

Joanne Rice

Cynthia Riggs

Dionis Coffin Riggs

Brooks Robards

Annette I. Sandrock

Valerie J.R. Sonnenthal

Ellen Martin Story

Jennifer Smith Turner

Holly St. John Bergon

Emma Young

William Waterway

Holly Wayman

Richard Weiss

Dick Weissman

Sally Williams

Warren Woessner

INTRODUCTION

We celebrate our 58th year in the art of writing poetry individually and sharing it as a group, whether we gather at Cleaveland House; or during the pandemic, on zoom.

We have met so regularly and often we seem to know each other's voices, and poems. With that knowledge we are able to address the poems with intimacy and care.

As Judith Neeld described our process in the last anthology, *Cleaveland House Poets 2013:* "Each poet reads his/her poem once, a volunteer reads it again, we discuss it, and move on."

What remains is a lot like archeology or if you will, fossil making, each poem another increment of the words we share. Pleasure given, pleasure taken.

> Poetry is hard work.
> To do it right, you need to surprise
> readers with language, ideas, and imagery.
> You can't fake it.
> Never explain.
>
> — Judith Neeld

It has been my greatest honor to oversee this incredible body of poets. The talent is formidable. The joy in sharing is palpable.

Thanks so much to Valerie Sonnenthal, Arnie Reisman, and Ellen Story for editing our new anthology. Enjoy all.

Fan Ogilvie, Facilitator
Cleaveland House Poets, 2021

Ellie Bates

salt air haiku

clanging bell buoy
rocks back and forth on waves
rhythmic sound of dawn

rays of sun rising
gleam golden on calm water
a day to treasure

vermillion tethers
wrap me in harbor's beauty
glorious comfort

day ends night begins
ruby billows ripple west
white moonstone shines east

for night

full moon light streaming
over dark tranquil ocean
a shimmering path

rest from all worry
follow where sky meets water
serene baptism

waves gently lap shore
music breaks the silence
hymn sung in salt air

moon my companion
I am a guest of the night
heaven my blanket

the art of noticing

the bud of a crocus pushes its purple head through February snow
orange marigolds of last summer reseed themselves in April's compost pile

strong wisteria branches with delicate yellow petals climb the garden trellis
peonies brushed red unfold near the butterfly bush, both welcome pollinators

gentle tide swirl washes onto shore, leaves pebbles like white pearls
threads of punky pink seaweed delicate yet strong grip a rock

thick line of a tree root twisted along an ancient way invites me to follow
red veins on cedar's fragrant bark, I touch it and remember mother's hope chest

many tiny plants grow in cracks of black asphalt on the bike path
lapis juniper berries hang on thin green needle boughs near the beach

a small acorn sprouts in a pine grove of the sanctuary, new home for a traveler
frogs among the pond's bulrushes and cat-o-nine tails croak a loud welcome

full moon streams into my bedroom, makes tree branches sway on the rug
gold sunrise through layers of clouds like the soft white pillow on which I sleep

tracks of deer visited last night and chewed the yew planted in my yard
silky webs of dew appear on cool wet grass in the morning, tents for fairies

let sleep come

let sleep come as worry keeps you awake
watch a full moon shine through the bedroom window

study tree branch shadows dance on the floor
count the number of times wind rattles the skylight

listen for cars speeding to make last call in town
pick up the book on your bedside table, try to read

hours pass ever so slowly, your eyes wide open
to check the orange lit dial on the clock, only 3 am

three more hours till dawn's light comes, still a long wait
close your eyes let your restless thoughts become dreams

dreams of not wanting the night to end when once
you were held close to a strong body and your head

in the soft pillow of his muscular arm kept fear away
remember his gentle fingers brush over your eyes

let the sleepy murmurs of his voice comfort you
hear him whisper your name again and again

let the lullaby of his love rock you to sleep

Masquerade

golden strands of sunlight cover your face
and hide the tears in your eyes

September once brought joy for a new school year
butterflies in your stomach fluttered in anticipation

now shadows of discomfort loom ahead
surrounding your life with blankets of fear

what was last year can not mask a sad reality
the new normal of ordering take out
social distancing, hand washing and face coverings
hides the smiles of family and friends you long to see
to hear their laughter, to sing and pray together

you are visiting behind screens, attend events virtually
pretend to be grateful for opportunities that fend off isolation
loneliness wears no mask and sits with you every day

graceful monarchs peacefully migrate west
while anxiety puts your travels on hold
another day passes, tomorrow still not risk free

cicadas sing from the meadow at dusk
a call to listen to their hopeful serenade
pure and free from the masquerade

solitude

I travel a dirt path laden with pine needles
newly fallen green oak leaves
some brown and dry crisp from summer drought
make a crunching sound
I walk between sparse Queen Anne's lace
and black-eyed Susan gone to seed
to the pond at Dark Woods

there I hear solemn honking of a lone Canada goose
is she calling to a mate? no answer
she circles between tall grasses
they bow to her like a royal visitor
through the rays of golden morning light
her cry interrupts the ping of acorns
as squirrels scamper and rush to hide them

from the path I watch her paddle round
I patiently follow her movement
she takes her time
has she journeyed from the flock to be alone?
no rush no agenda just a circling rhythm
I walk around the shore with her and listen
her cry is not desperate but an affirmation

I am here

the shore endures

whitewashed driftwood stand like bony sentinels
along a fragile path of dunes lined with broken snow fences
rivulets of sand stream between the slats
hardly stopping pebbles of soil that spill onto the barrier beach
massive cores of pines and cedars uprooted
erosion's testimony to the last nor'easter
a collage of kelp, limbs, spindly roots and pine cones
line the salt sprayed shore
eider ducks swim on whitecaps near the debris
white egrets nest in trees, left alone from nature's wrath
an oystercatcher dips its orange beak into the sand
still finds his meal of the day
I watch the sun shine on the opal water
walk near waves of tire tracks and follow the wrack line
fill my pockets with jingle shells, pieces of purple quahog
find hope to endure these troubled times

Tree Shadow

Sunlight dances in an enchanted forest
Paints a shadow of tree limbs on a huge boulder
Branches hug the erratic, protecting it

Solid it stands after its journey of thousands of miles
Rolling, rolling for millennia carried on glacial ice
Facing freezing weather finally uplifted on the land's moraine

Placed on a carpet of moss, it delights all who climb it
Slide down its lichen pocked surface without fear
Even swing from nearby trees onto this giant stone

The erratic becomes a safe marker where children meet
Where adults might find them or arrange their own gathering
To picnic, to wonder, to hope this place will always be here

Francesca Kelly

Outlaw

The guest room was desolate and bare
It would not be tempting to lie on that stale bed
With or without motivation
Gasping forget-me-not forget-me not
But she did lie there when she returned
Butchering the days not exactly living
Hiding in his the clues to all her loneliness
Till one evening
She dragged him into the drab room
Fierce with loneliness she hung him like Christ on the frame
Banging nails into the cloth as if her soul belonged to it
Wine stains on the carpet crushed into blood or roses
Slamming the room into some kind of order
Some kind of altar
Somewhere in her the knowing
That these acts that called for tenderness
Were far from tender
She will set him on a horse her outlaw Boer
She will paint his hands all over her
She will become addicted to rendering him live and inside her
And smear his face and tongue with blood
And the attar of her
In the spare room she is a chameleon
Consumed by colour
And something that was not there before
Calls out when she leaves

Like a live thing left alone
For her the room smells of oranges
Or the veldt or the sweat on the washerwoman's clothes
The sun brings first respite by day
Just as he sets at night
Day and day's end they tryst
Days and nights upended
Longing recedes and leaves them raw
Touch an absent anguish in their virtual release
Nothing quite holds them together
Words flare and are gone
Yet each by going back
Finds a way of going on

Light Fantastic

Neglect has flayed those empty rooms
All manner of desertions
Embrace the vacant space
No light sheds more gloom than neon

I take refuge in surrender
In my sleep I dream of waking
In waking hours my heart's asleep
Day and night roll into one
Life offers in great profusion
Confusion

Not far
Father and mother
Once a constellation but dwindled to a star
The naked eye a prison-cell
Nowhere the gate nowhere the door
Dim radiance
Indifferent and pure
Casts no shadow and loves the night

Ash stirs on the outgoing breath
The dancing motes beyond recall
We endure
Knowing somewhere
Landfall

Mourning sensation

You will not grasp its essence
Nor heed my naked feet without their ankle bells
Nor my quiet passions nor their faith
They will nowhere be found

Abide the ghosts in the lovers' room
To their ways you will resign
They will welcome you with chorus
They will welcome you thus
Give away her gowns give away her shoes
She has no use for her fragrant gowns
Take them down
Take them down and sit with us
She will dance no more in her sparkling shoes

Pied Piper

She goes barefoot
Her hair is a nest
And all the young studs
Think they know her best

Then he flying by catches her eye
Calls out will you come with me to the ends of the sea
To the end of time to the end of time
Will you come with me to the deep dark woods
To the end of time to the end of time
Will you come with me and be my bride
To the end of time to the end of time

She wipes her feet on the river-bed
And casts the prisms of her pride
To the silver moon all light inside
To the golden sun all dark inside
From the deep dark woods the song-birds call
From the ocean bed the sirens cry
The willowy veils turn to ash and die
As the wildling girl clasps him to her side
Her hair in her eyes and her laugh inside out
Suddenly cautious suddenly shy

She's a master of play a mistress of woe
A weaver of magic never in thrall
She lost herself to the knave in the pack
The piper the pan the ace in the hole

Too poor in spirit to mend his ways
He sends her gifts from across the sea
Playthings and relics and all sorts of things
He nails his dreams in a keepsake box
Along with the heart of this girl of mine

Seemingly careless never carefree
Ingenious in obliviousness
The barefoot girl with her heart in a box
Her hair in her eyes and her smile in knots
Weary of courage careless of hope
Patches the whole together again
While somewhere inside a throttled cry
Of winds and promises sweeping by
No more no more till the end of time
The end of time the end of time

Traje de luces

The matador
Resplendent in her suit of lights
Caught the scent of the young bull in the neon ring
And drew him in

Drew him in
Accustomed to other kills
He falters
Her laconic grace
Occultations of inscrutable intent
Igniting the field between them
The quickening pulse of blood
A rapturous tide in the heart of the amazone

She turns her back
Invincible

How often in her reverence to life
She surrenders to its twin
The brutal scars that adorn her fragile form
Livid in the lamplight of her solitary room
Her suit of light

She dreams of the moment when the ferro
Cleaves her heart in two

Peter Ledermann

Alaska

Thank God
We are so shortly here
So that there is a chance that we will not
Attempt to steal the Jewels from your Crown

Alaska

Do you see me behind the walls of my stateroom
Behind the walls of the jail I carry
on this tiny ship
Imprisoned far beyond the bars at the edge of the deck
Within myself
which gratefully, graciously cannot hold one small measure
Of your Grace
thankfully
it does not recognize
the smallness of me

Food for the moon indeed in this space
Evolved beyond impossibility
miracles of life
I just barely understand these newborn visions
But now I know the one secret reason
The Salmon must return
From so far off
To the doorway of forever
And I will return if I can find the way again
From oceans away

I never imagined such a beautiful woman
Whose eyes are the stars and moons melted
Sighted and elegant beyond deepest feeling
In her evening gown
Sequined with galaxies of alabaster ice blue
Would be so much more refined as her garments slipped off
My imagination
Into the sheath of the forever evening light

Alaska
I thank you for not waiting
for me
for making time itself forever
for replenishing my Faith
away from my kind
into the sunshine
of your night

Alien

If you were like me
You would go through your day like an Alien
Where the disconnected laugh of someone not too far away
had no relevance, except for its uniqueness
Where the insane beauty of a young brown gull, somewhat audacious
Follows you from the grocery store
Hoping you will drop something
Where the seemingly disconnected reach of every branch
of every tree, seems perfect in its filling up of space
Where every melting bit of ice pushed carelessly aside by the plow
is transforming from one state into the next
By every means possible

If you were like me - an Alien
The peaks of someone else's house that appear on the horizon
barely visible, would be someplace you would want to visit
Where the distant hills with their toothpick trees against the snow
nestled amongst the hills arranged by the Hudson river
Would look perfect, as the river current pushed down the blocks of ice
by choice

If you were me, you would feel like an Alien
When you wake up in the morning and your right arm doesn't work
and you struggle over the next 45 minutes
to try to get some alien control over this human form

If you were like me, feeling like an Alien when time does not advance
You would admire deeply
your grandniece
Who at two years old is directing traffic at the dinner table
and because she does understand far better than the rest
is telling everyone
it's not their turn
to sing yet

If you were like me, an Alien
You would question why the ancient instincts
Given to us to survive
Had not risen above our state of wonder
And become
Awe itself

Beautiful

Too beautiful to go back to sleep
The morning sprite before the sun
Black silhouetted trees that edge the world
Respeak stillness as night's undone

In quiescent twilight day is birthed
So perfect in its offering
Infinite outcomes by love conceived
Immaculately separate from our suffering

To taste the dew that's offered up
One would have to sacrifice
The comfort of one's darkened view
The tradeoff believed that will suffice

So it's a crow that breaks the dawn
Unravels peace that must unwind
And signals end to morning's birth
To usher deeds of manunkind

Too beautiful to be believed
Timeless in its continuing
Miraculous to be conceived
So fragile in its offering

Cut Flower

The day is before me
like a cut flower
As am I
And certainly you
To admire
To profess my desire
To keep
But I have stolen you from the garden
As if you were mine to take

As if anything is mine
But nothing
Save my faith
Truly is

And even that fades
When I am bent by the wind
Assailed by the events of day
Distracted from you
After a short time
Admiring

If I were
any kind of person
I would sit in the garden
Before you
All day

But the day is like a cut flower
Only to close at the end
To fall
To leave some petals
On the table
To remind me
Not to live life
Like a cut flower
In what will be
an empty vase

Deep Asleep

I prayed a small boy prayer
To see the invisible world that supports the visible
If only I could stay here in this place that is filled
With awe
The intense miracle of each day
Plants sucking water, birds supported by the wind
I want

Fish who wonder about air, us who wonder about nothing
Asleep
Asleep so deep in ingratitude
In near worthlessness
Spoiled children of earth, the Garden invisible
Look at those who have nothing now
That the shaking earth has taken back
Angry parent who punishes randomly because
She sets an example

All you have been given will be taken away
Far deeper than you
Deep asleep

So asleep
We don't accept the great gift of even being each moment
Inside of time itself
"If you are neither hot nor cold" It says
"I shall spew you from my mouth"

But I wonder if sometimes we are cold
So cold
We have been given
a second chance

Christopher Legge

The White Buffalo

In my ambling
Before trace arcs
Made their way
To my door

I was a seeker
In my dreams
Asking for the White Buffalo
To appear

A bold buffalo named Anger
Clouded my way
But behind, in the mist
A ghost appeared
From a place where trust
Lies in a nest, waiting
For us to discover

But here I was
Just a seeker
Amongst the mass
Meek afore the Furies

Then, the ghost
Came without my behest
Seasmoke
On a pond of forgiveness

She shook her head mightily
No...this one is not ready yet
Much to learn...

Then the White Buffalo was gone
Her entourage quick to follow
Nostrils flaring in the quickening gale

I hope to hear the buffalo's feet
Trample upon my dreams soon
I miss the steady beat

If I twere to dream
...And I hope to dream

I would understand
Not the White Buffalos' dismissal
More an invitation...that someday...someday
I might run with them

The Cloud Who Thought
He Was a Mountain

I awoke
And I was born
Mountain mists nurturing thunder's rumble
Knowing rain soon to follow
As residue of my favor

Colors emit
Flames ignite
Temblors quake
Amidst yellow's crackling fold

Life is bred
From elements of hot coals
And I...
I am mountain as any
Born as my brethren

No dolmen to lie beneath
As proof of death
More a penny found in the rain
Dust washed away
Revealing monument
As proof of life

But I am no mountain as any
I am Pharisee
Contemptuous pretender
Before the court
Of what I want to be

I am cloud
I am rain
I'm the beads that hang
From snowdrops in spring

I am more than mountain
And less
I am Orpheus never looking back
Broken lyre in pieces at my feet

And yet...
When I wake
Each morning found
Will-o'-the wisp Sun
Trying to break through
Pale's gray warning

I am born again
I am mountain

Aphor the Dog

I first met Aphor
While taking a walk
On Crystal Lake

She wagged her tale
And chased a stick I threw
We fell in love instantly

I asked around
And posted pictures
Of my way-word hound
But no one seemed to know
Or have met Aphor before

She may be dumb as a whip
But smart as a post and fence
Especially when a pair of bull terriers
From next door
Try to make themselves known...
Chasing them off is a story all its own

She's been the best dog ever
Only once did I have to take her to the Vet
They did an analogy on her
And said it would be prudent
If she had her allegories removed
It was a moral dilemma
We talked about it
And decided against it

A lesson learned
Is a pill we have to take
Every morning

Otherwise there's no meaning to life
A dog without an allegory
Might as well stay home
And chew on what's left
Of his or her own tale

I love my dog
I hope she stays with me forever
I hope she doesn't mind
My endless stories

I'm so happy
I took a walk on Crystal Lake that day
The Sun was just coming up
Over the horizon
Right before I met Aphor

Pathways

Ask me of riddles wisely expounded
And I'll tell you why
A hummingbird flies
A thousand miles
Just to turn around

But ask me why
I can't sleep unless
The ocean is in my ear
I'll quiver like a plover
And ask you
Have you never been?

To see the ocean...my ocean
When the Sun comes up
Angels dancing
Diamonds upon the waters

Or the applause of the quicklies
Saying goodnight for now
A reminder of the fire
Waiting at home

Have ye never been held up in her arms?
A tapestry 360
Awakening the clouds above
Pity the seeker who only wades
So close to finding love

Of other of life
I know a bit
Always knowing
Which way the wind blows
And when not
To keep a lantern lit

But ask me
If I could ever leave my ocean
And I'd ask you a riddle right back
Does the seagull fly high above the Bluffs
Just looking for food
Or is it just having fun?

The answer is both
One to keep the lantern lit
The other...ah, the other

Sit on State Beach
And watch the Sun come up over Chappaquiddick
Then we'll talk again
About the other

Georgia Morris

How softly

How softly we sat together in the car
at a dead end by the lagoon
watching the few boats
still moored in the March wind
his country music station on
to smooth the silence
For now, the cracked glass
of our sibling lives
flowed together like ancient
window glass, soft and running
twenty minutes to kill
before his appointment and
he wasn't hearing voices
he was being here now
having just eaten a cheese steak
napkin-wiped for the hospital
No voices screaming, nagging
no strangers yelling, Just
jump in front of the bus, Go!
Both in the front seat, here, now
we were full
March wind mesmerizing the water
and we, soft together.
Then Shania Twain finished
her ballad of heartbreak and survival
and he turned to me and said
Wasn't that beautiful?

I Lay in the Rope Hammock

I lay in the rope hammock
itchy with lichen from a year of neglect
the English ivy army ever encroaching
from the side, and from beneath
a cluster of annoying stems
poke at my waist

How did I not see
the marked ring of burial ground
the circle of hosta that surround
Sonia, Whiskers, Midnight, Brownie, George and Jack
to clutch their souls
dear dogs, guinea pigs and cat

Was it because the big boys were only ashes
and most of Jack having floated off
on the outgoing tide, that I forgot
their souls' planted spot?
And now I lay above to write, intruding
or seeking their upturned eyes?

It will be fine to feel the prodding stem
whenever their seeking ears need
a scratch, or I to hear
whenever their spirits move
in the earth we share, the hammock
swinging their soft touch back to me

Did I ever thank them?

Kiss the Spot

Why should she kiss the spot
he taps on his cheek
instructing her like an
expectant, leering uncle?

Does he not realize his
demand for her display
revolts her, but then
why does she comply?

The mystery of delayed rage
is a female thing
It trips us up,
and out of confusion
we tamp our own storm

I envy the women in Italian movies
who bark their anger
with wild abandon.
They slap, they scream
Can you imagine?

Movies are a wonder, but

how do we help our daughters to fight
the unwanted kiss with
instant fury
Is that asking too much
in the midst of young thunder?

A Telepathic Last Love Note

Inspired by a photo of parallel gurneys
in a Queens Hospital, March, 2020

our souls will collide
this I know
they will slide back into our intimacy
fused by tethered living
they cannot forget days
on the edges of land and sea
You will show me and I will follow
or I will hold out my hand and wait
weightless and no longer weary
and our souls will glide
magnetized by loving
to our light's center
and we will collide like atoms
and burst
putting ecstasy to shame
I so look forward to it, don't you?
silent and whole
a mist of delight
a balm of perfect warmth
a flow of peace
when our souls collide
and burst into everything
you and I will be home
we will be home
and always

What Kind of Rain?

For George Floyd

What kind of rain
is falling in the mind
of a nonchalant killer
knowing he is witnessed yet
drawn to fondle the
dust in his pocket

What is that drip staining
his twist of thought
before a crowd
The witchery of proud
power so delicious
he has to hold, to sip its spell

How can he dwell
inside such tainted gray matter
of fact so craven
his body can ease
in the calm of
such a hurricane

Jane

"How wonderful" she said
the butterfly returning to her chrysalis
so beautifully
it broke hearts

delicacy and grace en route
to stellar nebulae
beating the last of her glass wings
to mysteries
clearing the unseen
to make way
our aching blinding us
to her clear sight

Oh, Jane
you always wept at kindness
your wings glowed with pride
in us and we
thick with life then
told you The kids have arrived!
We're all here.

And out of your chrysalis
nearly consumed,
you rose, your self intact
to bestow your blessing
your last thought?
your last words to us,
"How wonderful."

I have a feather

I have a feather
the little boy said
I have a feather
I can fly

The others laughed at him
they didn't know
poetry

It rained and the boy looked up
to feel the rush on his face
while others ran inside

to watch a rain of
bullets on a screen
as the wet boy sang,

drops splashing his
eyelids closed,
better to see

I have a feather
and he knew flight
I feel the rain
and he knew joy
I have a song
and he knew power

While the others grew
to hear the music
wishing they could dance

buying entree to a concert,
the boy tuned his strings
to sing his song
And they, un-beknowing
met their idol
with applause

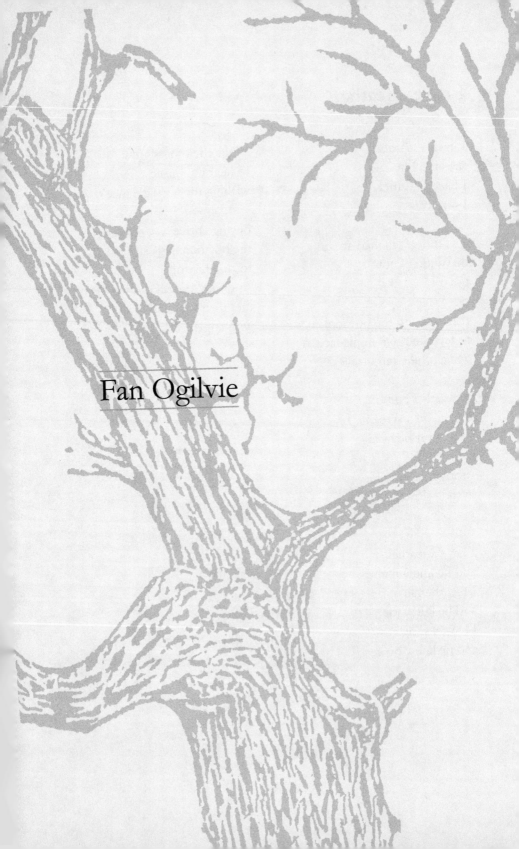

Fan Ogilvie

When You Almost Burn
Your Friends

It's a smallish island we live on.
In the northeast winter is the season
all year round—with variations.
Wood burning stoves or fireplaces
burn incessantly in most homes.

I lay wood for the evening fire
every morning on ashes of the night before.
Our island is lucky
enough to have two newspapers.
I am lucky enough to have paper to burn
for each fire. But I have noticed strangers'
faces on the covers of the newspapers
are the faces of very good friends.
This happens when you live here a long time.
I grab to wad the next ball of paper
And I see Justen Ahren, a very good poet
and friend, and behind him on the cover
of the next section is MJ Munafo. No,
I can't burn her either. At least not yet,
until I find enough headlines to set afire.

Is it cowardly or thoughtful to treat friends
this way? If I make any new friends
it is possible I will live chilled to the bone
but warm in the ways of few fires and friends.

My
Love

We after so many days
together are living the winter
life I wished for in the beginning.

A fire started & collapsed into
dark burning coals & ash,
quietly ravaged logs undressed

purr & hum or isn't it rightly
the fire & the wood spits
& hums together. Nothing wasted

yet all is wasted. It doesn't
matter much what we do anymore
If it ever did. You read most of the day,

get up for a bite from one of your
chairs. I glare into this iPad—a snailfish
from the floor of the ocean & walk

the dog in the ever noisy woods,
not with sound but voices of sight
the constant bleat of brown vs. green,

mosses siskin green velvet & minute
fern shapes. Ponds reflect not so much sky
as path & tree to make an earth

over time—effortlessly. Reduced to
our essential selves here beside
each other day after day our

murmurings noted & forgotten
like bird chirps/cracked twigs.
We move at night from near fire's end

toward a familiar bed still able
to stir dreams/snores. We sleep
laid as bark-charred/stripped logs

on a bed of coals red & darkening.

New England Lament

No, we do not have fifty names for snow,
but something widens and stretches the
word

we use to describe all forms of it: flakes,
beginning flurries, cumbrous clouds to an-
nounce

the arrival, snow piles, cover of white on
fields,
meadows, cities, bridges. Today, we check

the radar again, promises of the light light
substance—but no snow—still no snow.

Lear

She went on a tear this daughter of Lear.
Her nose was not clear this child of Lear.
Her iPad jumbles the letters she types
Is there someone in this house at night
The sly gene cries out with fright—
The odd astrologer's warning to say
She would end up friendless near decay
In the maid's room far away
Bleak and dark like a prison stay.
Not sure that she can now say
But that is how it is today.
She doesn't desire to travel the lands
Or the numbifying foreign seas—
Just stay home where she thought
It would be Walden Pond's Thoreau
A safe place to be alone.
She needs strategy to avoid this crone.

What does the world look like
Through her eyes real-time—
The leaves covering a forest floor
Daffodils six petals in clumps
Orange throats white bright yellow
She could match them to her paints
Colors bright however DISTINCT
From any thing we create except
Our children. A child has that
Alive feel and look—cellular.
And would you kill that—all
That breathes, including the daffodils?
As she picks them she hastens their death.

But where is this Lear thing going?

—A woman who ages
Is surprised by her bra her mirror her sex
Everything about her graying hair
Surprises her. A constant "not me"
Echoes again and again to twist
Her brain. She can't trust or control
Anything close to her. Eruptions
Slip out in damaging remarks like
Lear mistaking Cordelia's words—
When he desperately needs praise,
He hears condemnation
Of his worth and lovability.
Just when he decides to disembark
His ship is mutinied in his eyes—
Haven't acts of charity bitten
You in the bottom of your kindness?

There is that for certain.
Thunder lightning hail rain
Without stop grow peonies
Grow lilies grow ferns
Wet turkeys geese deer
To the bone. They shake it off.
We shake it on—betterthandeath
The 21st alternative to the 17th;
Weather the storm live the sea
Change and learn from not dying
Along the beachhead with your fool
Your wrested insight is too late—
Both have no arms left to fate.

The whole play is Lear and Cordelia
As in life it is only these two
But one needs a play in life—
One needs something to go to.
One needs more than early adoration
To sail a large brain through.
Notice the dead are more alive
Than any thing we make or cling to
Except the child. Only the child
Challenges the miracles of God
Who did not sacrifice his manmade ark
But rather his radical angel-born son.

When all elements mixed to become
First Life they took time
To breathe noxious air then oxygen
To become one thing and the next.
There should be great grand hurrays
For every creation from manta rays
To land and water hippopotamuses.
Earth outdid herself again and again.
Then there is man whose biggish brain
Carries weight, doubt, and insubordination.

Our mode of self preservation
Organizes for war and killing the other.
There is nothing like it in the universe.
There is no retaliation from any species
Except the smallest, perhaps the bacteria.
We know from ticks we can be laid low:
There are others more deadly to come.
It would be lovely if this grand retaliation

Had a purposeful causation—
Earth is pissed, God is incensed.
We haven't much time or we have much time.

When created Earth didn't
Know it had 4 1/2 billion
Years to go. As far as it
Is concerned it might have no end
Until the sun begins to die
At which time all that it is
All that we have done—dust.
Relativity and quantum gravity
In someone else's orbit for sure.
As for the long-tailed future—
Black holes will turn inside-out,
Evacuate worlds into the universe
And create new fresh ones to thrive.

Got a feeling that I can't let go
Got a feeling that I can't let go
Jamin the Van "Caught a ghost "

Susan Puciul

"Lo, such was her fortune....."
—Thomas Wyatt

a thousand days after he said
come into my bed and
show me who I am,

never
had the Queen looked
more beautiful.

she ate her crumpet
smoothed her dress
prayed with fervor

coins for the endgame
jingled in her pocket
as the procession
advanced on the cool May morn

to her right
the executioner
from France smelled
of freshly milled linen

good christian people
I have come hither to...
accuse no man

Anne thought it kind
of H to demand
only the most skilled from Calais

to refine the cut
not by rugged ax
but by bespoke sword

at the gallows her handmaidens
took great care in removing her
ermine cloak from the neck
she joked was "small"

good christian people,
I have come hither to die

the swordsman,
so skilled so swift

the maidens
tenderly gathered
her head
lips still moving with
all she never said

Visitation

I was ten
and flung upon a forest green
couch after a summer dinner
being bored

out of the dim
corner of the living room
where we watched Ed Sullivan
and Ponderosa the night before
a pulsing light

in blinding shadow
seen but not seen
seen truer than the truth
of the wallpapered room

gentlest breath robed in light
shifting to shock of the vividly Other
calling to live in what I thought
was me

called
to be deeply beloved
to be perfectly gone
it was terrifying
it was all I wanted

beckoned to let go of the entire
known world required
being gulped entire

I said a pale grain of yes
to the magnificent desert of it

after fifty years those ten seconds
are the pearl of great price
nestled and hidden
in the parched part of me

yearning for This
to seek me

again

keeper of innocence

mother
protect
your son barely two.
your outstretched hand
from the corner of the old photo...
I feel you beaming

he, in plaid shorts
tipsily perched on a flat suitcase
near the door reaching
to turn the knob

now sister,
open the door
into the June day
first step
out into a world
with no brother

we hadn't before
noticed an earwig
at a morning puddle
or the dandelion-fluffed
whiskers of our bony cat
or the busy spider
he would have
saved from swatting

grown man,
smitten by the voiceless
in grimy Yonkers parks

to the rescue of the shunned
and the lost
cat dog pigeon

every creature called
his tender heart
he chose the place
where his body would be
on a hill under a tree
where birds could
fall in love

mother
protect
from falling off a suitcase at two
from being slain by cancer at sixty

there is no protecting.
only being deeply here
until time becomes love
then swirls over the edge

until,
like pollen,
we all join in
the shining

Lita's Dream
After Anne Carson's *Each Day Unexpected Salvation* (John Cage)

sheen of sun on leathery leaves, sheen of bare bulb on needle,
sheen of nightlight on toddler's tooth, sheen of sea on girl from
ipanema, sheen of smashed glass on car in queens, sheen of joan's
hair in 6th grade, sheen of raccoon eyes in headlights, sheen of bright
cream on coffee, crow-black flying sheen, sheen iridescent on oil slick,
sheen shining from sacred heart of jesus, greasy sheen in ear of elder,
sheen of hooker bling on gun hill road, sheen yes on dew of morning,
sheen of fresh blood in war all wars, sheen of chant in dark places,
frizzled froth-of-waves sheen, sheen of clean colons, curving sheen on
peaches, sheen of vermeer's earring, tender sheen in chambers of the
flesh, martin sheen in Flipper's sheen, shouting sheen in new car lot,
sheen on sole of giotto's angel, sheen in pulsing mitochondria, sheen
on digital screens all over, sheen on slug in garden, sheen shot through
fog at shore

shining sheen o find us.

Andrea B. Quigley

All Time is Now

I danced with the wind last night
watched bits of gold in the sky
saw the leaves reflect purple in the pond
sat in a tree and screeched with the owls
watched slumbering children
grimace as visions of ogres
beset their dreams
felt the bulbs beneath the earth
struggle to rise
break through the earth
to breathe in the sun
I flew over the ocean
watched glistening mermaids
cavort in the waves hidden by night

I returned to childhood
touched my mother
pushing my carriage through the streets
saw the tiger lilies along the tracks
heard the clanging of the wheels
as we went over the coarse roads

I saw my father pruning his roses
plucking a giant beefsteak tomato off its stalk
saw him eating cake by the kitchen window
the sun reflecting blue in his black hair

The mourning dove cooed
I hung up my wings prepared for the day

Wasque

Black and white
With a tinge of red
An oystercatcher flies
Toward the mansion
Moved back several times
To prevent the ravages of the sea
A grey brown sea roiling today
In sync with an approaching storm
The sand not the white crystals
Of Caribbean islands
But homespun tan sand
That holds the boot prints
Of the dedicated fishermen
Who cast off the shore
Bringing bass and blues to the feast
Feeling like frontiersmen
Living on the edge
Joining the baby seal
Its iridescent head surfacing
To take a breath
And then descend

what heals you

the warmth of the sun
on your flesh
on a chill autumn day
the smell of the sea
carried on the east wind
shapes of animals or angels
in cumulus clouds
the heart connection
of a child's smile
the potential of being
loved well
the silent flight of geese
just because you looked up
a cherished friend sending
a winsome message
a hug or touch from
someone who
really sees you
the sound of canon in E
breathing deep
letting stress go
meditating
on all these gifts
in gratitude

comments on wearing
a new dress

you look like a cupcake
you're only wearing half a dress
maid of the mist
a canary
miss ruffley
ophelia
you look like the frosting on a cake
and i love sweets
a yellow jacket
where did you get that
(could be taken two ways)
i love it
it's different
silence and eye rolling
it was expensive
i thought of returning it
glad i didn't
look at all the attention
that has come rolling down
in my direction
just call me cupcake

Soaring

You know you can fly...
Don't you?

You knew it when
you were a kid
and went to the
top of the stairs
with your umbrella
you knew it in your DNA
until your mother told you
never to do it again

Soar
on your angel's wings
skim the tops of trees
play hide & seek
in the clouds
Don't believe
you can't fly

Look
at the dancers
those sleek Alvin Ailey ones
who leap six feet
into the air
when not performing
they hang out there
6, 9, 12 feet off the ground
chatting together, drinking tea
or
rise farther to kiss God's cheek

Remember
the tai chi master
whose students saw him fly across the room
he couldn't contain himself

Once
when my barriers were down
i flew
in the living room of a rental
on Martha's Vineyard
the family all dancing
to some forgotten strain

i lifted off
held aloft by the mystery
of belief
that
I
could fly

Mytoi

Set within a pine forest
Temple of meditation
Secluded world of Japanese elegance
Winding footpaths reveal welcoming
Birches camellias golden bamboo
An arched wooden bridge floats
Above a tranquil pool
Girded with yellow iris
Sounds of song birds, frogs, snapping turtles
A cacophony of ancient monastic chants
Mystical refuge
A place of peace
A sanctuary
To hear the souls whisper

Arnie Reisman

Translated from the English

I am in the cloud above the clouds
Crossed over in an afterlife café
A decor dedicated to leafy millennials
Walls of photos of what could have been
Designed no doubt by an ambience chaser

My father and I at a table for lunch
Truth was on the menu
We ordered

I meant to say please pass the pepper
Instead I said did you ever really love me?
Was it ever more than sharing blood?

He looked at me, eyes softened in revision
And passed me the pepper

He meant to say I need another napkin
Instead he said you have your mother's eyes
But you were adopted

I swallowed my pain, my pride, a few more peas
And handed him a napkin

The waiter came over and meant to ask
If everything was to our liking
Instead he said family may slake your thirst
But it always leaves a bad taste
He left the bill on a paper plate

I meant to say I survived the rest of my life
Without taking your fatherly advice
Instead I said lunch is my treat

My father dropped his knife and fork
And threw his arms around me
We both got up to leave and stared
Up there, there is nowhere to hide
In heaven it's all about subtexting

How It Went

Whenever winds seemed to waver
They moved like kites

She saw herself as Fanny Brawne
To his sickly sensual Keats

All that was available about her
Was the light coming from within

Each storm-less night a probing moon
Shone through a shadow of a man

A hand, the one not holding
The glass of delusion,

Pulled a calculated curtain
Across a pleated conversation

The difference between passion and
Obsession is the location of the wound

What the human eye can see and burn
Is one iota of it all

One Grecian urn in a sea of porcelain
Silence corrected a course unsound

Once more off to Byzantium
They moved like yachts

To him she'd always be Maud Gonne
To his prickly sensible Yeats

Dawn

My waking charmed, my hearing warmed
By the soft psalms of ruby-throated poets
Congregated to share the first new verse

For the sun on its morning tacking over the line
Who then fly off, celebrated by the crested
And tufted, back to their treetop desks

My inner eye tested,
Heart lifted, feathers rumpled,
I waddle downstairs to mine

Immaculate Degeneration

"We are here on Earth to fart around. Don't let
anybody tell you any different."
— Kurt Vonnegut, *A Man Without a Country*

You are here only to make a clean getaway
To violate with shod feet
To waltz through ballistics

To keep the Sabbath where it belongs
In hanging gardens of Babylon, whether
On Long Island or on Spoon River

You are here only to suffer
For everyone who came before
So take steps to dance to it with abandon

You are here to show you've been chosen
To play heartstrings, play irresolute
To give off the scent of state perfume

If you were able to hear only
If you were predisposed to speak justly
You would not swap natural for ritual

From the first yawn you begin to be gone
Everything becomes flexible
Becomes fodder

Did you perform miracles and caesuras?
From a distance are those wings on your shoes
Or just shreds of toilet paper stuck to your heels?

Animals play hide-and-seek
Play tug-of-war, winner-take-all
Sports are who we are

We cannot live without prizes
Your first friend is a stuffed animal
Your last is the animal you've become

Pillows of Wisdom

While waiting for an aggrieved god
to pick up America
and shake it by its ankles
I fulminate

I contemplate how we got here
I won't be impolitic and ask questions

A dog abused by excuses for democracy
I lift my leg on the grave of answers

Man cannot find peace if he remains
robustly committed to equivocation

There is no antibiotic, no cure
for the nausea of silence

Morals can be found only
at the ends of fables

Every nuance shivers
in the coldness of interpretation

Every ruin was left by righteousness
on its way to greatness

My country, right or wrong,
could not make up its mind

Brooks Robards

The Old Dog

We summon her to the park
following her demented trot
in the wrong direction.

She no longer can climb
into the rear of the car
unless she walks around it
once to clear her brain.

Other dogs, on their outings
and curious, do not interest her
although she sniffs their traces
yellow and pungent-scented
leaves behind her own.

Her journey is a circular one
for her as well as us. She refuses
to leave unless we join her at once.

Some days she stays at home
happy to do her business
in the backyard, barking at
imagined animals, even birds.

No longer able to climb stairs
to the second floor, she pants
to live, at least for now.

Avian Melodies

I.

Birds chirp, tweet
twitter, a wall
of sound blocks
the commotion of cars.

They celebrate their nests
their eggs, the flood of light
that the new season brings.

II.

A flock of birds
like a wave of angels.
Such dancing gracefully
like synchronized swimmers
Busby Berkeley or Rockettes.

They settle in a tree
swoop down into the yard.
Then gone in a minute.

Paper Doll

In those March days when I lay
in bed with unexplained
fevers, Betsy McCall was
my companion. I scissored
her free from her magazine
page, but only after
my mother brought me
magazines. Little did I
know I could have mailed
away for cardboard copies.

Today I would park those
on the shelf above my bed
let Betsy's clothes distract
me from the pain of broken
bones, once again confined
paper thin, in a sickroom
waiting to walk again.

Bardo

The sweet death
that follows
day's end is
filled with images
we call dreams
disconnected stories
from that other
world we long for
as we practice entering
into the sacred infinity.

When light returns
so does renewal
but slowly because
we are not ready
to rise and enter it
lying instead, half
returned, remembering
with eyes closed
what came before
welcome to remain
in death's darkness.

This death a prelude
to the one that escapes
with the body that held
the spirit, freeing it to
wander with others.

Leaf Glow

In death's awful beauty
October foliage doubles
the luster it gathered
over longer, warmer days
into colors that heat up
the lengthening shadows.
On the dimmest, rain-filled days
they glow, a trick confounding
what we know happens next.

Leaves cascade in wet and wind
strike gold against blacker trunks.
Until branches bare themselves
for the coming freeze, they hold on
to those matchless, mortal colors.

The Beggars of San Miguel

They curl up on the narrow sidewalks
in the shade like caracols. Wrapped
in their rebozos, these women have no limbs
except the hand that reaches out as you walk
down from the Parroquia and El Jardin.

How many pesos can they collect
from the gringos before heading
back to their villages in the campo?
They must do well. My five-peso offer
for a photo earns languid dismissal.

In their wisdom they know
my few dineros will not
free them in this lifetime.

Good Friday

Not holy this year, only
a celebration for the dead
and for those not dead
but afraid, wearing masks
wearing gloves, staying
six feet apart. This the cross
we all must bear, without
redemption, bodies stacked
in freezer trucks, buried
in fields not cemeteries.

We hope for life as we
once knew it, not the same
an end that does not come.
We walk, watch TV, call
friends to wish them well
make sure the virus
has not taken them. Let
us hope for the resurrection
following this dreadful day.

Annette I. Sandrock

Footsteps of a Leaf

Footsteps of a leaf
roll down the street
as I drink coffee
in a yard where my bird feeder waits.
Morning sun and breeze in opposition,
my left side burns, the right cools.

I note braver birds as they land—
cardinals and sparrows
alert to my stillness.
Are they smart or foolish?
Life full of contradictions
resonates with nature.

I sit up straight, into the sun,
while my lover faces head down
to still cool ground.
Squirrels watch and wait.
I meditate,
prepare for battle of finality.

Covid rages overhead.
"Not in the air," they say,
but lingering on enemies
that portage it,
former friends unwillingly enlisted
for its propagation.

Friends are enemies to be shunned.
While tongues speak, lips move,
sounds emanate
behind individualized masks of creation.
Creation itself feels on pause
as minds race with fear or solutions.

Lack of knowledge becomes the norm
and the queen of all is confusion
to be brought down by a coup over flu,
rebels and the distraught.
All's frozen
in a wake of paralysis.

My Flower Closes

My flower closes for a while.
A retreat from lack of sun
has caused my petals to wilt,
my dew to lift.
I must close tight,
go inward brave
to view what exists
that no man knows.

Not to worry—
darkness can be no worse
than what light has not brought.
Not to desert you, no never—
I leave you with a cloak of love
to don or doff as you may wish,
for your wishes in the end
are all that matter.

Hope has floated.
Black birds flock
to watch my ascent or my demise.
In the end, all turn white,
and white, the hottest flame of all,
engulfs blues,
burns sweet and swift,
my love.

One cannot lasso hope.
It floats, sways with the wind,
momentum not from self
nor Gods or Goddesses.
It springs from rare desert streams,
surrounds itself with pales of smoke.
A force unknown unto its self,
it pairs with luck, not fated.

And so it is with love.
Love strikes freely,
its hand seen and felt,
not its will.
I live in its shadow
and its light.
I hold fast, though
its presence is in constant flight.

My flower reopens when I feel
warmth of sun, spit of rain,
caress of bees on my stamen.
Those elements allow me to brave
storms, pandemics,
all threats,
to imagine
my fate as eternal.

Surviving Covid

Winter holds opaque black
that keeps the world hostage
inside its darkest dream,
one that makes the nightmares
of childhood pale as a spider web in shadow.

Man prepares in vain by counting possessions,
trading those that lost their value,
collecting only what he imagines
will act as refuge or defense
against an enemy that strikes while hiding.

The hollowness of life is perceived,
a disease that was carried all along
through vanities of thought and egos of deluge.
It is impossible to halt movement of this scourge
as it is preconceived by unseen demons.

The only hope is somewhere unknown,
to be discovered, uncovered by change
imposed by the very evil that makes it necessary.
Humanity waits, whispering prayers to Gods hitherto unknown,
previously called upon for smaller tasks.

Where are the miracles promised,
the ones that lift and save one from ill fate?
If they exist, only through unknown acts
can they be forthcoming
to heal these sores that festered for eons.

War mongers created weapons to enslave, to rob,
to control others perceived as weak or evil.
Now all turns against us as we breathe in deeply the backfire of our folly.
Our thoughts entangle in past solutions
that can barely serve as tourniquets.

The answers are within and without,
so obvious they're invisible.
We overlooked the obvious for centuries,
chose the easiest, greediest ways
to build a world only meant to support in the short run.

Now, facing the serpent of repent,
we are given the means to discern
an enlightened path, or free will to keep the old.
A crossroads of rip tides, not mysterious, but treacherous
must be navigated to save ourselves.

Forest of Wisdom

As we walk an ever narrowing path
lined by trees of knowledge
whispering living secrets,
we suddenly trip,
only to drift forward
like leaves from some primeval mother.

Falling, rocking side to side,
we land softly on rich ground
to deposit our truths
as gaps between trunks
close to form a solid wall
between us and our former dream of the world.

Once void of wind,
this stand now fills with it.
We climb, whirl,
intertwine with late blooms of summer
alight the highest branches.
Here time passes, marked only by seasons.

We witness flowers wilt,
petals join as they depart
to carry seeds of wisdom,
lessons hard-learned, hard-earned
down to root in this forest's floor.
There, sprouts will provide spring tendrils.

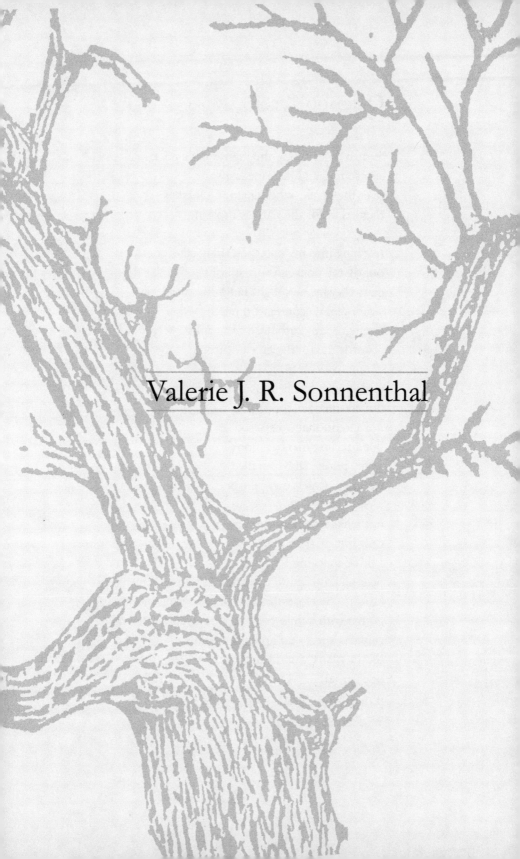

Valerie J. R. Sonnenthal

Quansoo Creek

Sunday brisk along the high water's edge
sun setting and just one last shot
over the creek standing among leashes
reigned in for the narrow crossing

reaching into my bag something slips
out of my pocket a soft splash
glass slices water   light fades like a shadow
a moment disconnects time
I watch as my turquoise case sinks
towards the murky creek bottom

underwater scenes replay accidents
not accidentally dropped
nor intentionally disposed of
but a feeling of liberation
as my phone slowly settles
resting between two pilings

not a fisherman in sight
only out-of-state plates
I drive checking for gear
near pick-ups parked outside lit homes
head to the closest fisherman's house I know
armed with a milk crate on a rope and a leaf rake
sun sets and I end up lying down
on the plank wood bridge and still cannot reach
one car left ... Wendy's head lamp and Rob
now reaches the rake in a too strong current
we give up for night

sunrise is a riot of pink and blue skies
tide too high to try
outfitted by Captain Tilton
I return and move the net
down easily reaching bottom
between rocks, shells and seaweed
not a hint of turquoise, dragging
side to side, climbing onto rocks
reaching across silt into water
familiar and new—the current pulses

severed from distraction into a quiet
I barely remember—silence my friend
no need to know if I'm carrying
my phone has drowned
dearly departed
in a scene film worthy seeing it replay
slowly calmly disappearing severing
my deepest connection only to return
home my son insists it is time to let
the apple fall and take the reins of the bison
after five years of never feeling smart enough
to have figured out any more than I needed
I will let go no status quo just an android
and I will walk again across the Quansoo Creek

Not Locke, Descartes or St. Thomas Aquinas

No truth
 exists outside the self.
No self
 exists outside the truth.

even an ontological fool
both believing in reality
a conceptual truth
in truth non-existential
by and by
a definition of god
existence of non-existent
things like God or God itself
it is an Island an island
it exists like god
in hearts and minds
the people know
their island their hearts
their lost minds
fluid in lost words
God a thing rammed

down throats, shadows
beyond clouded ways
there are questions
all answered unsaid
an echo of something
sacred like truth
lost at sea
seen refrigerated
truck after truck
like piano keys
only the black keys
laid in bags
truth not counted
film never lies
narrative fiction
pulped through streams
screens scream exclusive
dreams deny the elusive
a precondition for conceiving
one white world exists
truth enough for some

Bonding in Poetry
for ABQ

you appeared one Wednesday
at Cleaveland House
poetry bonding us like blood sisters
your serious humor
counting breakups
your sly warm smile welcoming
mischievous with words
always an anchor of community support

You and the Sun Port—ABQ
Albuquerque and Andrea
coincidences we slowly uncovered
in poetry we may stray
you always lead us home
you gave unwittingly
your support, love and gentle kindness

Andrea of Catholic Queens
your words strung like a rosary
each poem a prayerful offering
finding your truth,
willing to split memories open
delve to the beat of all life
simple dramatic succinct

grateful to share so many Wednesdays.

Do You Know

do you know me
do you know how it feels when you can never hide
do you know what I eat for breakfast
do you know my father has been dead 59 years
do you know I can't speak German
do you know when you first heard "Never tell a lie"

do you know me
do you know me by my "big hair"
do you know me by the profile of my nose
do you know my family
do you know they lived in their homeland 500 years before they
        could own a home or land
do you know I could not eat alone in public for 50 years

do you know me
do you know me because my mother walked naked around our third
        floor apartment
do you know the NW corner of 72nd Street and Lexington Avenue
do you know how many construction workers whistled or cat called
        me growing up
do you know that man in the beige raincoat with a pair of men's
        pants hanging from one forearm
do you know what happened in the bushes by the Egyptian needle
        statue in Central Park when I was six

do you know me
do you know I ran up Lexington Avenue barefoot in a downpour
do you know I was 12 when I first tripped

do you know Ritchie Haven's manager's family always got high
    with me after babysitting
do you know how many vanilla frozen custards I consumed from
    Central Park
do you know the Different Drummer was the first place to get
    jeans like rock stars

do you know me
do you know enough
do you know how easily I slid between the visible hidden in plain
    sight
do you know the magic that happens when you prepare food
do you know the power of the night sky
do you know what I did to breathe for many knotted years

Kora

is to remember
the sufferings of all beings
walking round
the stupa
the temple
the monastery
living prayer
in each step
walking through heaven
with buddhas
teachers
smiles
and greetings
between offerings
amassed weathered
and those being left

Tibetans walk clockwise
we follow in their steps
up steep climbs
gravel, mud, stone
to terraces in the clouds
temples in caves
temples in stupas
temples in stone
om mani padme hum
home in prayer
home in heart
home in being
present

one step at a time

fingertips tingle
near 18,000 feet
slowly making our way
past construction
to a path
worn by twelve centuries
echoes of prayers
in the wind
rippling from flags
carved into stone
pressed into clay
hushed into breath
after breath

Ellen Martin Story

What's your Talisman,
if not a Mask?

that back-in-the-drawer rabbit's foot?
grandmother's crucifix?

the beach?
a two-for-one—
the great healer, salt-water,
drown for the full preventative,
bake in the sun for rewards
of cancer

alcohol?
a disinfectant to be sure,
but if you drink happy until
you sway, stink, slur
you'll repel whoever
comes near

the gun?
combined with the mask
you can shoot anybody
who is or isn't wearing one
depending

Witness

In memory of O.W.C.

I see you, barren maple
as you release your final
crimson leaf and with a tear
that transforms and freezes,
swirls and settles on
a snow-covered lump
of stone. I witness your
grief creation, now
a diamond-studded ruby,
dazzling in twilight, pinned
onto an ermine cloak, your
mourning becoming majestic,
your lesson, my reconciliation.

That Pretty Girl

The black-hatted walker who shadows
her shadow home from school—*pretty girl*
let me in. Run up front stairs, lock
door. Some other warm kitchen
brews peace. She, like a broken-reeded
clarinet, just a squeak when the black
rotary phone rings each 2:15, handle
weighted with hot coal as another ghost
prompts her to disrobe slowly and describe.
She crawls up attic stairs but a smaller room still
hears fears. A slit of dusky sun slinks across
floorboards, a hornet stings her palm
as she pulls down one more shade.
She worms into a corner, her forever.

Patsy

Patsy, a puppy pure Doberman,
my father thought was springtime
perfect, my Mum thought was
a stalled winter-storm. Sophomoric
Patsy, who one day sought
adventure and a year later, Dad
found on the leash of another man.
Dad called to her—Patsy, come!
but she parted the troubled air
only half-way—
preferring the call of a new name.

The cat died next
the end of any more pets.
Mum was the broom handle
Dad leaned on. She swept
away sorrow. Then
emergency savings, kept secret,
burned in the homestead
stove pipe.
Mum swept those ashes
into a small paper-bag
she stored on a counter,
stupidity's reminder.

"For the Love of Money"

Song written and composed by K. Gamble, L. Huff
and A. Jackson Recorded by the O'Jays, 1974

Amen died from multiple
gun shots to the soul.
Not in a pew of holy worship
or at an altar of divineness,
not at bedside asking for forgiveness,
nor at even-song or matins, Amen
was shot on Wall Street,
his raised palm tattooed,
"peace be with you."

It is not known where
Amen will be laid to rest.
His will be a pauper's grave,
until an ecumenical council
determines a location and structure
for visitors' fees and souvenirs.
A simple plaque will be inscribed
"May Amen Rest in Peace."

Amen is survived by a 9th-
degree great grandson, Letitbe,
last seen decades ago playing violin
for a Beatles tour until,
it is rumored, he eloped
with Eleanor Rigby to live
in a yellow submarine submerged
somewhere off the coast of Bali.

According to the New York Times,
Amen's will was found
in the bowels of the Vatican's
St. Peter's Basilica in a book
of Handel's Messiah, translated.

The will is said to stipulate that
Amen's name, as the last word,
cannot be used without royalties
for an estate yet to be confirmed
because in November 2016
he had himself copyrighted.

The perpetrator of the crime
has not been identified.
Amen's last words were said to be:
"Let him and me be free so we can
finally make some money!"

'Round Midnight

Waking or awake still I thought I
understood sleep's nocturnal paths—
the rhythmic patter of rain or sometimes
counting backwards. Instead tonight,
uneven snares of wet and wind
march on my skylight with vigor.
And while I begin to slide around
this mud-bathed cerebrum, forums
form that debate
ad nauseam injustice's nature.
Later when the sky's drums
have marched away, the skylight
black and quiet, I imagine outside
where I could be cold and numbed
until unconscious. But too lucid
at 3 a.m., so invoke Alexa: *play
'Round Midnight,* again and again
'till the last I hear are notes
of a sorrowful muted trumpet.

Jennifer Smith Turner

Color of Language

He thought it was safe
To finally say—ain't
Proud man
Crayola skin
Licorice-stick color
Most leave in box for another

Little did he know
World said—no
Slang—you—will not go
O.K. for majority lawyer
Sportscaster, entertainer
Symbol—engaged in the world
Not you brown-eyed child
For you accusation
less than—outside—foreign—street

He thought it was safe
To finally say—ain't
Without skipping beat

Little did he know
World still said—no
Ain't gonna dis us so
We who taught you to speak

Dis—what?
Now he knew it was safe
To finally say—ain't
But I no longer want to
Been stolen from me
Not going to speak like thee

Little did he know
World would say—ho!
Say it ain't so
Licorice stick thinks he better than we?

He thought it must *finally*
Be safe to say—ain't
Assuming he was free

Little did he know
World said—hell no!
It ain't so
Will not be

He sighed—
Perhaps for the children
If not me.

Safe and Sound

When we had it, we didn't think about it
it was simply there, sure as clean air, running water
we wrapped ourselves in its comfort with as much ease
as slipping into deep sleep, warm covers gently pulled over our heads
soft pillow inviting us to let go, give in
we heard stories of how others do not have it, saw images
of other's absence of basic comfort, surety, take-it-for-grantedness
but we—we had it, the denied ones were so far away
faint apparitions of loss, disappointment, infringement
easy to wipe from our eyes

Nowadays, we no longer have it
not as clearly as before
not as assuredly anymore
apparitions take solid form
mirror images of those
with whom we are intimately acquainted

Like Love

We proclaim our love the ultimate emotion
it is with us in happiness
soothes us in moments of despair
tempers us in the face of anger
it is the reason we said "I do" 19 years ago
as we stood with family and friends
to profess our declaration of paramount love

It guided us through sorrowful farewells to our parents
through transitions from professional life to retired life   to Island life
guides us still through the evolution from middle age to old age
from good health to bodies challenged by years and gravity

It enveloped us on smooth or stormy seas
while visiting countries around the world
it was always our love that made it possible
for us to be comfortable as strangers in strange lands
for people to welcome us without the benefit of common language

But what if our love is actually the penultimate emotion
discovered after spending months in a pandemic lock-down just the two of us
bumping into each other in a large space that somehow seems smaller
hour by hour day by day week by week month by month
when our conversation at breakfast is—what's for lunch
while having lunch—what's for dinner—while having dinner asking—
what will we do for the rest of the evening...

This claustrophobic existence in our beautiful bubble has helped us to appreciate
"I like you" is the ultimate sentiment that keeps our love like love

Whale Watch

We think we're watching her
she who coaches her calf in feeding ritual
birds fly closely overhead
cheer the young one on
their survival tied to life's lessons

mother lifts her tail from crystal waters
spins up around twists for us to observe
each side in its elegant fluidity
then thunders deep under the surface
sends food shooting into the air

mouth wide teeth bared
she grabs startled fish
fills her cavernous cavity
gestures to calf—your turn
do as I have done

however imitation—not quite
as imposing as the original
birds sing support for much smaller ripples
appetizer-like samplings
thrust into the air

mother's show over
deep deep down she plunges
glides beneath our boat
we run to the other side
expectant of further demonstration

watching watchful
she whistles spit up to the sky
faces us
winks
bows

calls to her calf
dives
races away
hump in view
tail flickered

Daughter's Wish

I believed unfailingly
you had no visiting rights
forsook her for others
left us for ones yet to be born

I stood with her
as you walked away
mother's pain—daughter's

My nephew, your grandson
close by your side at the end
he now wishes
for more time with you

My wish—
better use of time
I did have

Warren Woessner

Message from David

After the diagnosis
I told you, "Now I know
what's going to kill me."
Of course you disagreed
but for once I was right.
When we last spoke
I told you not to visit—
no long good-byes,
so instead you told me
how busy you were,
a big shot patent lawyer
on the board of Legal Aid,
working with researchers
to save many I knew from AIDS,
traveling to conferences but,
you said, only ones where
you would be "important,"
at least for the time
it took you to dissect
some law I'd never heard of.
Once, I told you I wasn't afraid
any more of not being able to write
another poem, and then after
each long call I would ask
"But are you writing?"

Cleaning Up

I wash the dishes
and think about the little girl
in the ad who says, "What
does the dishwasher do?"
She means the machine,
of course. I know
what I'm doing here

and so did Luis,
who for years washed dishes
in a Sanibel restaurant.
He always sent money back
to "his wives" he called them,
and got jobs for his nephews
in Fort Myers.
He rode his bike
to work every day
until his sight failed
and he returned to Mexico.

A U.S. citizen now
and an honored elder
of his large family—
"a man of judgment."
The clan had even brought him
an almost new pickup truck,
that he'd never seen
and didn't know how to drive.

Too Young to Go Steady

Nat King Cole, 1962

Charlene was my date
for the Valentine's Day Dance,
"February Fantasy."
I thought I loved her.
She was between Guy and Allen.
So the time was right
and the feelings were warm
in my average desolate teenage life.

We drove her brother over
to pick up his date, Joy.
They had just started going
all the way. He went up
to get her while we waited forever
in the orange glow of the hi-fi
in her father's dark den

When a tune rose up
on a glossy voice hanging weightless,
filling in the space
between our lips with the words
she wouldn't I couldn't say.

The dance was pretty and dull.
We sat at pink card tables
before a velvet-coated band
that couldn't play rock and roll
or much of anything else.

But, driving her home,
a fog bank hid the road—
hypnotized her I guess
since Charlene let me kiss her
goodnight for a long time.
though I didn't really know
how to get the most out of it.

I know better now
and I still love that voice.
Thank you Charlene and Joy
and thank you Nat for singing
"Too Young to Go Steady"
that night in 1962.

Poem for My Father, Still Alive

Why not write it now? My memory
wont' improve. These days
we get along O.K.
What I care to say
just fits a poem.
Not much, but still all
yours and mine.

I remember the endless auto trips.
You said don't read! look out!
here's what we came to see—
God's country.
Now I can't recall the books.
The mountains still are clear as hell.

And you didn't help my "unhappy childhood"
but neither did I.
You made me turn the B's into A's
and took the A's for granted.
Yet when I wrecked the Rambler
you kept it hid, said
the girls might not date me
if they heard I was reckless.
No sweat. They didn't anyway.

I have to say we've got a lot
in common: bad eyes, kidney stones,
a stubborn skill at hiding affection.
We fight for too many convictions
to defend.

The holiday truces always broke down.
Tact and tolerance were for the weak.
We left our wounded behind
and fought on
like elk with antlers locked,
starving.

At last I learned to wait you out.
Age will tell, is telling.
Dad, you've had to accept
things that won't change:
your body breaking down,
the tears and love escaping, free
at last. "Give peace a chance"
I used to say.
It's not so bad, I guess,
it's us.

Taking Both Roads
Considering "The Road Not Taken"

can make all the difference, Mr. Frost.
In fact, it may lead to more divergences
than you'd ever expect or imagine.
But you were gifted and you took
the poet's road and stayed on it
all the way to reading for the Kennedys
on that cold inauguration day.
I watched you on T.V. then went right back
to reading the *World Book Encyclopedia*.
It's strange that my various life is as full now
as my desire to find my first path was then.

2021 Cleaveland House Poet Biographies

Ellie Bates, retired from the Edgartown School, is member of the Martha's Vineyard Museum, Cleaveland House Poets, Martha's Vineyard Poets' Collective, Martha's Vineyard Poetry Society, New England Poetry Club and PathwaysArts. Her collage work of images and words has appeared at Featherstone Center for the Arts. Her writing has been published in the *Vineyard Gazette, Martha's Vineyard Times,* and *Cleaveland House Poets: 50 Years.* Her photographs and poetry are in her three small chapbooks: *Everything Changes, Rooted in Change* and *A Collage of Poetry* and in work by Howes House Writers and the MV Poets' Collective. She is honored again to contribute to the 2021 Cleaveland House Poets anthology and is grateful for the opportunity to walk in nature on Martha's Vineyard which inspires her poetry. She thanks the community of writers on and off-Island for sharing their talents with her and continuing the mission of healing and hope through words, especially during the Covid-19 pandemic.

Francesca Kelly is a jack-of-all-trades, artist, and choreographer of equestrian theatre. This group of poems is dedicated to her daughters Melissa and Amber, her grand-daughter Anouk, and dear friend John Harwood, who has always encouraged and loved her writing... She thanks you with all her heart.

Peter Ledermann is currently owner and director of Engineering at the Sound-smith Corporation. He has spent much of his life inventing as well as designing and manufacturing all types of high-end audio equipment including the "lost art" of hand making and rebuilding phono cartridges. He also worked for many years at the IBM T. J. Watson research center, a "think tank" located in Westchester county New York. His interests include philosophy, humor, all forms of science including metaphysics, travel, writing short stories and poetry, but most of all gathering with friends. He is a member of the Cleaveland House Poets and has published one book of his poems, illustrated with his own water-color paintings. His poetry has been published numerous times in *Cross Currents* magazine and appeared in the last Cleaveland house poetry anthology. Peter has been "spontaneously" receiving poetry since he was nine years old, and states that he just "quickly writes what he hears." Once he receives them in this manner, he generally remembers most of what he has "heard" over more than 60 years.

Christopher Legge is a grateful member of Cleaveland House Poets. Chris has been honing his unique genre of "story poetry" for years. Many poems are taken from the sights and scenes of the gift that is living on the Vineyard. As well, Chris lets in the embers of the Olde Country burn bright with deep gratitude. Chris is very close to publishing his own book of stories, *A Whither in the Twile: A collection of rhythm and rhyme,* he hopes you will enjoy.

Georgia Morris has been writing poetry throughout her life — while workshopping plays at HB studios in New York, writing documentaries for ABC, PBS, TNT, and AMC, raising her kids in Tisbury or writing plays or independent films for Galen Films, her production company with her husband Len Morris. Poetry has been her secret garden nourishing every one of these outward lives. And now, having finished her first novel, and been invited to join Cleveland House Poets, her poetry is crawling out from under the bushel, where it has been thrown to accumulate for too long.

Fan Ogilvie published *"YOU" selected poems* and *Knot: A Life,* a memoir in 2008. In 2016 *Easinesses Found: Poems and Paintings* was published, receiving special recognition from the Washington Independent Review of Poetry and Grace Cavieleri, creator of the Poet and the Poem series. Fan taught English and poetry in Washington, DC; New Haven, New York City, and Martha's Vineyard. She was selected to be the second Poet Laureate of West Tisbury, MA. She worked three years at the Dukes County House of Correction, where she published two volumes of poetry by the inmates. She is now facilitator of the Cleaveland House Poets, the oldest continuous poetry group in the USA. Fan, also a painter, had a one-person show at Featherstone Center for the Arts, the Free Library of West Tisbury, and the Chilmark Library. Fan and Arnie Reisman co-edited a collection of Judith Neeld's poetry in 2019. In 2020 she published *The Berth: American Themes in Poems and Images,* a conversation between a contemporary poet and a passenger on the *Mayflower* 400 years ago answering the question what has happened to the dreams between then and now in America.

Susan Puciul wrote her first nature poem when she was nine in the wilds of Bayonne, New Jersey. Her experience has been that poetry begins in the body and she has combined her poems with choreography performed at The Yard in Chilmark, at Featherstone and with the dance collective, What's Written Within. A member of the Cleveland House Poets since 2009, her work has appeared in their second anthology, in the book, *Legacy of Light,* on NPR and in various poetry journals over the years. Her day job has been running Tashmoo Realty for thirty-five years and raising four children in the home she shares with her husband in Chilmark.

Andrea B. Quigley (1941-2017) Andrea Quigley, an accomplished poet, essayist, teacher, and business consultant, was a longtime resident of Martha's Vineyard where she actively participated in multiple community-oriented organizations that included the Cleveland House Poets, the Martha's Vineyard Poets Collective, and the Martha's Vineyard Poetry Society. Andrea also served on the boards of the Featherstone Center for the Arts, and the Friends of Family Planning; and was affiliated with Women Empowered and Peace Quilts for Haiti. Following Andrea's death, a well-attended celebration of life memorial ceremony was held in her honor at Featherstone..

Arnie Reisman, Martha's Vineyard Poet Laureate (2014-2016) is the author of three books of poems. His comedy, *Not Constantinople,* had its world premiere at the Martha's Vineyard Playhouse in 2015, directed by MJ Bruder-Munafo. His documentary, *The Powder & the Glory* (the Helena Rubinstein-Elizabeth Arden business rivalry), co-produced for PBS with Ann Carol Grossman, became the musical *War Paint,* featuring Patti LuPone and Christine Ebersole. It ran eight months on Broadway in 2017. He's also a columnist for the *Vineyard Gazette* and lives with his wife, Paula Lyons, on the Vineyard. Since its debut in 1996, he and Paula have been regular panelists on NPR's comedy quiz show, *Says You!*

Brooks Robards wrote her first poem in third grade, then exploded into life as a poet while working on an M.A. in English at the University of Hartford. She has been writing poetry regularly ever since, producing five collections in collaboration with artists. After earning a Ph.D. in communication at UMass/Amherst, Brooks taught journalism, film and women's studies at Westfield (MA) State University for 21 years. Five of her fifteen publications are poetry. Brooks lives in Northampton, MA, and spends the summer months on Martha's Vineyard. The natural world is frequently the theme she pursues.

Annette I. Sandrock, resident of Marthas'a Vineyard for over 30 years, published her first book of poetry, *Labyrinth* (2019) in Portugal and is honored to be registered in the National Library of Portugal. Her book, exclusively containing her poetry and images of pruned treetops of Crete, is carried in several book stores in Portugal as well as on Martha's Vineyard. The images from *Labyrinth* have taken on a life of their own, having been shown at Island libraries and virtually by PathwaysArts of Martha's Vineyard as "an instrument to raise awareness of the personality and special sentience of trees, our companions and providers." Through manipulation of her photographs, Sandrock uniquely captures trees as embodying spirits and personality traits of humanity and animals. Her writing and poetry have appeared in several Island anthologies as well as several Martha's Vineyard publications.

Valerie J. R. Sonnenthal started writing poetry at age 12 after finding a small notebook on a dusty California road, something she has never stopped carrying with her. When she moved to Martha's Vineyard in 2005 she was fortunate to be invited to join the Cleaveland House Poets. She has had the pleasure of participating in poetry readings at the Featherstoone Center or the Arts, Martha's Vineyard Playhouse, PathwaysArts, and local libraries. Her poems have appeared in the *Martha's Vineyard Times, Rattle* and two previous Cleaveland House Poetry books. She is a regular contributor to the *MV Times, The Local* and *Martha's Vineyard Arts and Ideas*. She owns Peaked Hill Studio, teaches biomechanical yoga and offers sound healing. Valerie lives in Chilmark with her family and beloved dogs.

Ellen Martin Story began enjoying Vineyard life as a small child and has been writing poetry for over 40 years. A resident of Oak Bluffs, where she and her husband retired in 2014, previously, she was a human resources administrator for the MBTA. Several of her poems have been published in the *Martha's Vineyard Times* and she has read for the Martha's Vineyard Playhouse Poetry Café as well as PathwaysArts. She is thankful to have been welcomed into the Cleaveland House Poets and to be a part of this 2021 anthology.

Jennifer Smith Turner is is an award-winning author. Her debut novel *Child Bride* has won several literary awards including the Best E-book for 2020 by the Black Caucus of the American Library Association and Biblioboard, and Winner Next Generation International Indie Book Awards in African American Fiction. She is the author of two poetry books: *Lost and Found Rhyming Verse Honoring African American Heroes* and *Perennial Secrets Poetry & Prose*. Her poems have appeared in numerous publications including the *Vineyard Gazette* and the *Martha's Vineyard Times*. Writing a novel has been a wonderful journey for Jennifer, however poetry is a part of her soul. She lives in Oak Bluffs with her husband Eric.

Warren Woessner is a poet, an avid birder and a patent attorney who splits his time between Minneapolis and the Vineyard. In 1968, he co-founded *Abraxas* magazine and WORT-FM and hosted its poetry program. His poetry has appeared in *Poetry, Poetry Northwest, Epoch, Iconoclast, 5AM* and the *Vineyard Gazette,* among others. Many collections of his poetry have been published, including *Clear All the Rest of the Way* (U. of Nebraska Press), *Our Hawk* (Coffee House Press) and *Exit-Sky* (Holy Cow! Press). Warren has received fellowships in poetry from the National Endowment for the Arts, the McKnight Foundation and the Wisconsin Arts Board, and won the Minnesota Voices Competition sponsored by New Rivers Press. His poems "Message From David" and "Cleaning Up" first appeared in the online literary review *On the Seawall.*

ACKNOWLEDGMENTS

Cleaveland House Poets exist today thanks to Cynthia Riggs's unwavering support of continuing the tradition her mother Dionis gave birth to—whether in the parlor by the fire or sitting outside with grazing guinea hens, turkeys and chickens. Although we have not been able to convene together for nearly a year none of us would be here without Cynthia's support.

Cleaveland House Poets also thank Featherstone Center for the Arts, all the Island libraries, the Martha's Vineyard Playhouse Poetry Café and Pathways Arts for their continued support allowing CHP to give voice to their words to share in public. We also would like to thank both the Martha's Vineyard Times and the Vineyard Gazette for sharing poetry, ours and others, with our community. Lastly CHP thanks the West Tisbury Library for hosting the Dionis Coffin Riggs Day of Poetry held annually on her birthday, August 6.